A Taste of culture

Foods of Thailand

Barbara Sheen

KIDHAVEN PRESS

An imprint of Thomson Gale, a part of The Thomson Corporation

THOMSON

GALE

Detroit • New York • San Francisco • San Diego • New Haven, Conn. • Waterville, Maine • London • Munich

© 2006 by KidHaven Press. KidHaven Press is an imprint of The Gale Group, Inc., a division of Thomson Learning, Inc.

KidHaven™ and Thomson Learning™ are trademarks used herein under license.

For more information, contact
KidHaven Press
27500 Drake Rd.
Farmington Hills, MI 48331-3535
Or you can visit our Internet site at http://www.gale.com

LIBRARY OF CONGRESS CATALOGING-IN-PUBLICATION DATA

Sheen, Barbara.
  Foods of Thailand / by Barbara Sheen.
    p. cm. — (A taste of culture)
  Includes bibliographical references and index.
    ISBN 0-7377-3037-4 (hard cover : alk. paper) 1. Cookery, Thai—Juvenile literature. 2. Thailand—Social life and customs—Juvenile literature. I. Title. II. Series.
  TX724.5.T5S44 2006
  641.59593—dc22
 	
                                                                        2006000247

Printed in China

Contents

Chapter 1
Land of Plenty   4

Chapter 2
Delicious Flavors   16

Chapter 3
Snacks and More Snacks   28

Chapter 4
Sharing Food   40

Metric Conversions   53

Notes   54

Glossary   56

For Further Exploration   58

Index   60

Picture Credits   63

About the Author   64

Chapter

1

Land of Plenty

"This land is thriving. There is fish in the water. There is rice in the field,"[1] an inscription on a 700-year-old Thai tablet proclaims. Thailand has always been a land of plenty. Anything and everything grows in its fertile soil. Its coastal waters and many inland waterways are filled with fish and seafood. Thai cooks have an abundance of foods to choose from. But it is three ingredients—rice, fish, and chili peppers—that Thai cooks cannot do without. Thai meals are incomplete without them.

A Part of Thai Life

To the Thai people, rice is not only the most important food on every table, it is a part of life. In Thailand, rice

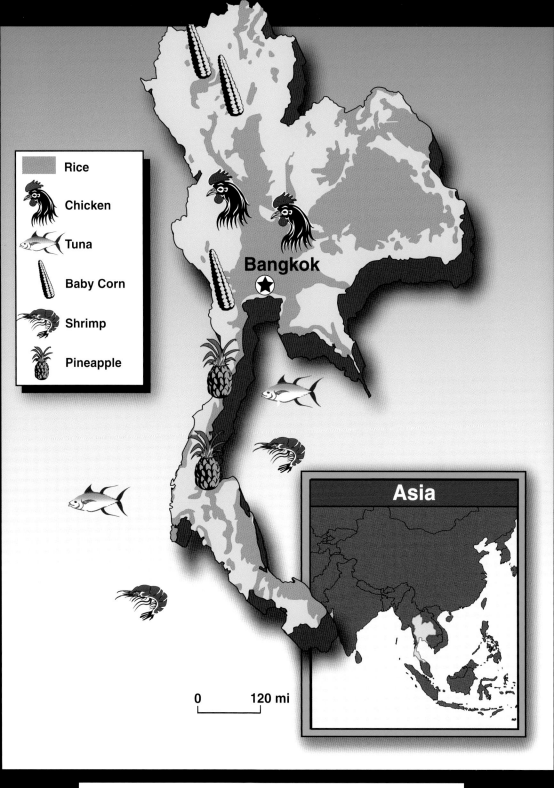

Rice

Chicken

Tuna

Baby Corn

Shrimp

Pineapple

Bangkok

Asia

0   120 mi

Food Regions of Thailand

A woman removes dirt from rice by sifting the grains back and forth.

is associated with a person's well-being. In fact, when people greet each other, they say: "Have you eaten rice yet?" An answer of yes signifies that all is well.

Thais have been growing rice for more than 5,000 years. Archaeologists say that the Thai people were the first in the world to cultivate the grain. Today, rice fields

Lemongrass

Lemongrass is a popular ingredient in Thai cooking. Lemongrass is a type of grass with a bulb-shaped base. It has a light, lemony scent and flavor.

Lemongrass is used in Thai cooking in two ways. The bulb, or root, which is too tough to be chewed, is often cooked in soup and stews. Before it is placed in the cooking pot, the cook bruises it by pressing on the bulb with the side of a knife. This releases lemony oils and adds a citrusy scent and flavor to whatever it is cooked with. Since the bulb is inedible, it is removed before eating.

The stalk of the plant is edible. The outer layers of the stalk are tough, but the inner layers are delicious. These are sliced or minced finely and used to flavor a wide range of Thai dishes.

Lemongrass adds a citrus flavor to many Thai dishes.

that produce more than 20 million tons of rice annually carpet Thailand. And 40 percent of all Thais make their living growing or selling rice.

Thai farmers grow many different types of rice, including jasmine rice, which is considered to be among the finest rice in the world. This transparent, long-grained rice not only tastes wonderful, it smells like a bouquet of tropical flowers. Jasmine rice is the most popular rice in Thailand, and Thai cooks prepare it with care. First, they thoroughly rinse the rice to remove dirt and excess starch. Many Thai cooks use an electric rice cooker to steam the rice. Others prepare rice the old-fashioned way, boiling it and then letting it simmer for at least twenty minutes. Then they uncover the pot to reveal the light, fluffy, and fragrant grain.

Mounds of Rice

Thais love the delicate taste of rice. Every man, woman, and child in Thailand eats about 1 pound (0.45kg) of rice per day. The centerpiece of a typical Thai meal is a large, lidded bowl piled with rice. Small bowls of meat, fish, vegetables, and spicy sauces accompany it. Diners scoop mounds of rice onto their plates and top them with a splash of sauce and a few tidbits of meat, fish, or vegetables. Chef Kasma Loha-unchit explains, "Instead of having a little bit of rice to go with the meat, the Thai way is to have a little bit of meat to go with the rice."[2] Thais do not eat this way because there is a shortage of other foods but because they adore rice.

Rice

Jasmine rice is the most popular rice in Thailand. It can be purchased in most supermarkets or Asian grocery stores.

Ingredients:
2 cups jasmine rice
3½ cups water

Instructions:

1. Wash the rice by pouring water over it and rubbing the wet grains between your fingers. Repeat this process twice.
2. Drain the rice. Combine the rice and 3½ cups water in a pot. Cover the pot and bring the water to a boil.
3. When the water boils, lower the heat to medium. With the cover still on the pot, simmer the rice for 20 to 30 minutes, until most of the water is absorbed.
4. Turn off the stove. Let the rice sit in the covered pot for 10 to 30 minutes.
5. Carefully uncover the pot. Hot steam will escape. Fluff the rice before serving.

Serves 4

Outdoor fish markets are available for cooks who do not catch their own fish.

Thais eat rice at almost every meal. In addition to being the main course of most meals, rice is also the main ingredient in many soups. It is also used to make flour, which is turned into light and delicious noodles and sweet treats.

Plentiful Fish

Fish and seafood are a perfect accompaniment to rice. Thai cooks have a wide variety of edible water creatures to choose from, including bass, catfish, carp, sardines, shrimps, lobsters, eels, and crabs, to name a few. Thailand has 1,683 miles (2,709km) of coastline and miles of rivers, canals, lakes, and streams, all teeming with life. Many Thais own small rowboats, and fishing is a popular pastime. In fact, over half of all Thais regularly catch their own fish for meals. Some Thais dig ponds in their backyards, while others raise catfish in barrels or large plastic buckets.

Since so much seafood is available, it is not surprising to learn that fish and seafood are important staples in every Thai's diet. Thais are as likely to eat fish or seafood with a mountain of rice for breakfast as they are for lunch or dinner. Thai cooks prepare fish and seafood in many ways. They steam crab claws, whole fish, or shrimp and stew fish in sweet coconut milk, the liquid that is extracted from fresh coconuts. They wrap sea bass in banana leaves and grill them over an open fire and panfry squid. They grind fish to make fish balls, which they cook in soup, and mince shrimp to form delicate shrimp cakes. They turn mussels into pancakes and stuff **prawns** with ground pork. There are almost as many fish and seafood dishes in Thailand as there are cooks. According to author Jennifer Brennan, who lived in Thailand, when it comes to fish and seafood, "it is conceivable that one could dine for a year . . . and never repeat a specialty."[3]

Thai Salt and Pepper

In addition to eating fish and seafood at almost every meal, Thais use a liquid drained from salted, fermented anchovies to make **nam plah** (num pluh). This flavorful sauce, which smells and tastes as fresh and salty as the ocean, may very well be the most important ingredient in Thai cooking. Thais use nam plah in much the same way that Americans use salt. Kasma Loha-unchit explains: "In my kitchen, fish sauce is used liberally in place of salt to flavor all sorts of dishes—appetizers, snacks, soups, salads, curries, noodles. . . . In short, everything but dessert."[4]

Nam plah is also the basis for dozens of different dipping sauces. At least one or two of these sauces accompany every Thai meal. Among the most popular is **nam prik** (num prick), a zesty mix of nam plah, shrimp paste, roasted red chilies, garlic, lime juice, and sugar. Tasting spicy, salty, sweet, and sour all at the same time, nam prik has been called the taste of Thailand. Indeed, in Thailand good cooks are distinguished by their ability to make nam prik.

Hot and Spicy

Using chili in nam prik is not the only way Thais use their favorite spice. Chili peppers add color and flavor to Thai cooking. Sixteenth-century Portuguese traders brought the fiery peppers to Thailand from

Children and Hot Foods

Although chilies are a favorite Thai food, Thai children are not given food seasoned with the hottest chilies until they are at least eight years old. Thais say that a young child's tender taste buds cannot tolerate extra spicy foods, so enjoying the spiciest of dishes is considered an adult pleasure. When a child acquires a taste for the hottest chilies, the child is considered to be growing up. Eating such dishes is an informal rite of passage, just as drinking coffee is in the United States.

A boy sells cooked meat on skewers. Meat cooked with spicy chilies is eaten only by adults.

Latin America. Like almost everything else, the peppers grew well in Thai soil and added a zestier flavor than traditional black pepper to rice and fish dishes. It was not long before the Thai people adopted the peppers as

Hot and Sweet Nuts

Thais use chili every chance they get. This tasty treat gets its hot and spicy flavor from red bird's-eye chili. Jalapeno chili or crushed red pepper can be substituted. Cashews or almonds can be added to the mixture or substituted for the peanuts.

Ingredients:
1 cup peanuts
1 tablespoon honey
¾ cup shredded coconut
1 bird's-eye chili, seeds removed, minced
1 teaspoon peanut or other vegetable oil

Instructions:
1. Heat the oil in a frying pan.
2. Stir in the honey. Add the peanuts and coconut. Cook over medium to high heat until the nuts are browned, stirring constantly.
3. Add the chili pieces. Cook for 1 minute, stirring well. Serve warm or at room temperature.

Serves 4

their own. Today, hot chili peppers are the backbone of innumerable Thai sauces. In fact, an old Thai saying proclaims: "Chilli is Thai, and Thai is chilli."[5]

Thais grow about a dozen different types of chilies, but three—bird's-eye chili, sky-pointing chili, and banana chili—are their favorites. Bird's-eye chilies are tiny, bright red or green peppers. Measuring only about 0.39 inches (1cm) in length, these peppers are among the hottest chilies in the world. Daring Thais eat them fresh and whole as well as dry them to make fiery red and green **curry** (cur-ree) sauces. Sky-pointing chilies are also used to make curry as well as other sauces. These somewhat milder red, green, and yellow peppers are about 2.36 inches (6cm) in length. At almost 4 inches (10cm), banana chilies are the largest and mildest of Thai chilies. Besides using them in sauces, Thai cooks often pickle these red and yellow peppers and add them to salads and noodle dishes. They add not only vivid color but an irresistibly zesty flavor.

The tastes of spicy chilies, pure aromatic rice, and fresh fish arc hard to resist. Although Thai cooks have an abundance of ingredients to choose from, it is no wonder that they cannot do without these three important ingredients. They are an essential part of Thai cooking and Thai life.

Chilies

chapter

2

Delicious Flavors

Thai cooking is delicious. Traditional Thai meals blend five essential flavors: spicy, sweet, sour, bitter, and salty. Many Thai dishes are a delightful mix of all five tastes, while others emphasize just one or two. But when these dishes are combined, they characterize Thai cooking. Thailand's favorite dishes—curries, soups, and salads—reflect this delectable mix.

Curry

The Thai word for curry, **gaeng** (keng), literally means a liquid thickened with a paste. Unlike the dry, yellow powder that is sold in the West as curry, Thai curry is a stewlike dish that starts out as a spicy paste. Although

Thai curry is a dish made from a spicy paste, coconut milk, meat or seafood, and vegetables.

Eating in Thailand

Unlike many Asians, Thais do not use chopsticks except when eating noodles. Long ago, Thais ate most foods with their fingers. Some foods are still eaten this way. But since the 19th century, forks and spoons have been used.

Thais never put a fork directly into their mouths. This is considered bad manners. Instead, Thais use forks to steer food onto spoons, which are placed in the mouth.

At informal meals, a roll of paper tissue is usually placed in the center of the table. Diners rip pieces off the roll and use them like napkins.

At formal dinners, cloth napkins are common. Towels dipped in ice water and scented with jasmine flowers are presented to diners after the meal so they can wipe their hands and faces.

Most Thais use metal utensils rather than chopsticks at mealtime.

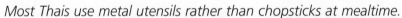

curry is often associated with India, Thais have been making their own version, which is thicker and uses more fresh ingredients than Indian curry, for centuries. In fact, most Thai cooks have family recipes for curry that have been passed down for generations.

Making Curry Paste

To make curry, a Thai cook first places chili peppers, nam plah or shrimp paste, and a mixture of herbs such as lemongrass, basil, and garlic into a stone bowl known as a **mortar**. Then, the cook pounds the mixture with a small, wooden, clublike tool called a **pestle** until it forms a thick, smooth paste. Turning fibrous herbs and chilies into a smooth paste is not easy and takes strong hands. Some modern Thais use a food processor to save time. But traditional cooks say that pounding the mixture by hand is the best way to release flavorful, fragrant oils from the ingredients. That is probably why, according to Jennifer Brennan, "In **Bangkok** [Bang-cock], every morning, one of the first sounds heard is the 'thunk, thunk,' of wood hitting earthenware or stone, as the day's spice pastes are prepared."[6]

After the paste is smooth, it is boiled or fried in co-conut milk. A creamy, scrumptious sauce forms. Depending on the recipe, other ingredients such as bits of chicken, pork, beef, fish, seafood, or vegetables are added to the sauce, which is spooned over a mound of rice.

By varying the combinations and proportions of herbs, chilies, and additional ingredients, Thai cooks create a multitude of different-tasting curries. Yet there are similarities. The chilies make the curries hot. The herbs add a hint of tartness and bitterness, the fish sauce or shrimp paste provide saltiness, and the coconut milk adds sweetness. And, no matter the combination of ingredients, all Thai curries have a deliciously pungent aroma.

A Perfect Match

Thai cooks carefully match the herbs and chilies in their curries to complement the other ingredients. Every Thai cook has favorite combinations and recipes. There are many different types of Thai curries. Red curry is among the most popular. Its strong flavor and vibrant color comes from dried red banana chilies, lemongrass, garlic, fresh turmeric (a bright yellow spice), and shrimp paste. It is often combined with beef or pork and vegetables. Then there is fiery green curry, which goes well with poultry; mild and sweet massaman curry, which is matched with beef and fruit; and slightly sour orange curry, which is paired with succulent shrimp. No matter the combination, chef Patchara Pornipitatong explains, "the depth of flavor and intenseness of curry pastes make everything you use them in taste wonderful."[7]

Uniquely Thai Salads

Yam (yum), or salad, is often served with curry. Thais make many kinds of salads and enjoy them as a side

A large selection of chilies and herbs allows shoppers to mix and match flavors.

dish as well as a light meal. Thai salads are different from those served in North America. Besides containing leafy vegetables, they usually contain meat or fish, herbs, chilies, sour fruit, fish sauce, rice, and nuts. They are often served warm, and are always finished with a highly seasoned dressing that enhances the many flavors and textures of the salad's ingredients. Chef David Thompson explains: "Thai salads are versatile. They can be enjoyed at any time of day, in any circumstance; as a snack, an appetizer, or to accompany a bowl of comforting rice soup."[8]

Bok Choy

Thai cooks are as likely to gather salad ingredients that grow wild along Thai waterways and fields as they are to purchase them in a store. Popular additions include edible flower petals, watercress, basil, cilantro, carrot tops, celery leaves, mustard greens, citrus leaves, and bok choy, a type of Asian cabbage. The greens are combined with paper-thin strips of cooked beef, pork, fish, or seafood and slices of sour green fruit such as mangoes.

The salad is served already dressed. One of the most popular dressings combines

Beef Salad

Beef salad is popular among Thais. This recipe calls for deli roast beef. Barbecued beef or slices of steak can also be used.

Ingredients:

1 pound deli roast beef, sliced into thin strips
1 small sweet red onion, chopped
$\frac{1}{2}$ cucumber, peeled and cut into long thin strips
8 large lettuce leaves
1 stalk lemongrass, finely minced
1 tablespoon Asian fish sauce
Juice of 1 lime
1 teaspoon sugar
1 teaspoon crushed red pepper

Instructions:

1. Place the lettuce leaves on the bottom of a platter, so that they cover the platter.
2. Put the lemongrass on top of the lettuce.
3. Add the meat, followed by the cucumber and onion.
4. Mix together the fish sauce, sugar, and lime juice. Pour the mixture over the salad.
5. Garnish with crushed red pepper.

Serves 4

lime juice, nam plah, sugar, garlic, and green banana chilies. Once dressed, the salad is garnished or decorated with still other tasty treats that are often cut to form dainty flower shapes. Oranges, limes, crushed nuts, coconut or chili flakes, mint leaves, or bits of ginger all are common **garnishes**.

Beef salad is one Thai favorite. It is a combination of barbecued beef with mint and citrus leaves, spicy dressing, and an onion and chili-flake garnish. Green papaya salad is also popular. It contains a mixture of shredded green papaya, dried shrimp, peanuts, mixed greens, and a zesty chili-lime dressing. The final salad is an artful blend of beauty, delicate fragrances, and the five essential flavors.

Multi-Flavored Soups

Soup is another dish in which Thais mix different flavors. Thais make hundreds of kinds of soup, which they eat at almost every meal. Unlike people in the West, Thais do not eat soup as a first course. Instead, soup is served with the rest of the meal and, when accompanied by a large bowl of rice, is often a meal in itself. As a matter of fact, a hearty bowl of soup is a favorite Thai lunch. Jennifer Brennan explains: "At noontime in Thailand everyone stops and flocks to little food shops. . . . Gaeng Chud Look Cheen [fishball and mushroom soup] is among the most frequently ordered soups during these lunchtime breaks."[9]

Most Thai soups start out as a clear broth, or **stock**, made with water and beef, pork, or chicken bones. The bones provide a rich flavor and are removed before the soup is served. Fried garlic, lemongrass root, galangal root—a bitter herb similar to ginger—and lime leaves perfume the broth and add a unique sharp taste. The last three herbs are unchewable, so Thai diners must carefully fish them out of their soup.

Artistic Foods

Thais love beauty in all its forms. They especially like richly decorated things. The elaborate designs on Thai temples are an example of this. So is the way Thais carve fruits and vegetables into different shapes.

Thai cooks are adept at creating works of art from food. They like to decorate salads with vegetables, chilies, and fruits cut into the shapes of flowers, fish, and birds. They garnish soups with cucumber peels that they carve into delicate leaves. They hollow out pineapples, pumpkins, papayas, and melons, cut them to look like ornate baskets or boats, and fill them with rice or salads.

Working with food in this manner takes patience and skill. A sharp knife is also essential. The beautiful results make the job worth the effort, however.

A woman carves melons into intricate flower shapes for a mealtime display.

Chicken and Coconut Soup

This popular soup, known as Tom Kha Gai in Thai, is a creamy chicken soup. To make it spicier, add more red chili flakes.

Ingredients:
1/2 pound chicken tenders
1 12-ounce can coconut milk
3 cups chicken broth
1 teaspoon crushed red pepper
1 stalk lemongrass
2 slices ginger
1 tablespoon sugar
1 teaspoon salt
Juice of 1 lime

Instructions:
1. Pour the lime juice over the chicken tenders.
2. Mince the lemongrass stalk.
3. Put the chicken tenders, ginger, and lemongrass in a pot with the broth. Cook over medium heat for 40 minutes.
4. Add the coconut milk, sugar, salt, and red pepper to the soup and stir. Cook on low for 10 minutes. Serve with rice.

Serves 4

Once the stock is made, Thai cooks add a variety of ingredients. For instance, fish balls made from ground white fish and egg whites are formed into spheres similar to meat balls and added to chicken stock, along with mushrooms, pork strips, rice, nam prik, and green onions, to make fish ball soup.

Prawns are a main ingredient in hot and sour soup, one of Thailand's most popular dishes.

Hot and sour prawn soup is another favorite. It gets its sour taste from lime juice, which is blended into the stock. Then, fiery bird's-eye chilies, plump sweet prawns, tomatoes, mushrooms, bitter herbs, and a splash of nam plah are added. The result is a fragrant blend of the five essential flavors. That may be why hot and sour prawn soup is one of the most beloved soups in Thailand. According to Kasma Loha-unchit, "It is the most popular soup in Thailand. . . . No menu is without it."[10]

Just as hot and sour soup is a wonderful blend of ingredients, all of Thailand's favorite foods are a delightful mixture of flavors. Whether eaten alone or in combination, the results make every meal a treat for the taste buds.

Chapter

3

Snacks and More Snacks

Thais love to snack. In fact, most Thais eat five or six times a day. Everywhere, food vendors offering every snack item imaginable set up food carts, which usually open at dawn and close after midnight. Other vendors, pulling carts on foot or with bicycles or motorcycles, go door-to-door. Enticing aromas fill Thai streets. "At times," according to Joe Cummings, a frequent visitor to Thailand, "the streets in Thailand look more like food fairs than thoroughfares."[11]

Each vendor has his or her own specialties, and the range of choices is tremendous. Hot noodles, sizzling fried fish cakes, coconut pancakes, soupy banana pudding, and juicy barbecued meat are just a few of the freshly prepared treats. And although the vendor's carts are often modest, the food they offer is so delicious that people from every walk of life enjoy their wares.

This mobile feast has been a part of Thai life for centuries, and may very well be one of the earliest versions of fast food. Among the favorite offerings are boiled and stir-fried noodles, **satay** (sah-tay), and fruit treats.

Rice, Egg, and Bean Noodles

Noodle vendors can be found on nearly every Thai street, as well as in bus and train stations, on piers, and in boats floating in Thai canals. Chinese immigrants who settled in northern Thailand in ancient times

Outdoor vendors display foods with flavorful aromas as Thai shoppers pass by.

A Thai cook lifts a strainer of noodles from boiling broth.

brought noodles with them, and Thais have been eating them ever since. Thai cooks make three distinct types of noodles: egg, bean thread, and rice noodles.

Delicate-tasting rice noodles are made from rice flour and water. Rice noodles are usually sold in a block that cooks cut into strips before cooking. The resulting noodles can be long and wide or as thin as toothpicks. Yellowish egg noodles get their color from eggs, which are added to the flour mixture and give the noodles a rich taste. Bean thread noodles are clear, gelatinous threads made from mung beans and water. They do not have a distinct flavor, but rather pick up the flavor of whatever they are cooked with.

Sticky Rice

Glutinous or sticky rice is a popular snack food in Thailand. When cooked, the chewy grains tend to stick together in a lump, which is how the rice got its name. Many Thais eat sticky rice with their hands. They break off bits of the rice and roll the rice grains in the palms of their hands, forming them into a little ball. Then they dip the ball into spicy sauce. Although this sounds messy, it is not. The sauce sticks to the rice, and the rice grains stick to each other rather than the diner's hands.

Sticky rice is also used in sweets. Thais cook it in coconut milk and serve it with fresh fruit. Thais also grow black sticky rice. This rice has a nutty flavor and is often used to make pudding.

Boiled or Fried, Wet or Dry

Thai cooks boil or stir-fry noodles to make many tasty treats that hungry Thais snack on day and night. Boiled noodles are cooked in a strainer immersed in broth and served either wet or dry with a choice of meats. Wet noodles are served in the broth they are cooked in, while only the broth that sticks to the noodles is served with dry noodles. Eager snackers make their selection by specifying the type of noodles and meat they want and whether they prefer the dish wet or dry. In either case, the noodles are piled into a bowl with bits of boiled beef, pork, chicken, or duck, or meat or fish balls.

Stir-fried noodles, on the other hand, are softened in water and then rapidly fried in hot oil with different ingredients. **Pad thai** (phat tie), one of the most popular of all Thai noodle dishes, combines rice noodles flavored with nam plah, sugar, eggs, chopped peanuts, and garlic with shrimp and bean sprouts. Because it takes about five minutes to make, pad thai originated as a quick and nutritious snack for busy office workers in Bangkok.

Garnishes

Whether snackers choose boiled noodles or pad thai, they top their choice with dozens of flavorful garnishes that are arrayed in small covered dishes. There are hot and salty pickled chili peppers, nam prik, granulated sugar, lime wedges, sweet basil, red chili flakes, chopped peanuts, and green onions, just to name a few. Since diners choose their favorites, adding as much or as little as

A chef prepares an enormous pot of pad thai noodles in a Bangkok marketplace.

Chicken Satay

Satay is not difficult to make. It can be made with beef, chicken, or pork.

Ingredients:
4 chicken breasts, cut into 12 strips
3 tablespoons soy sauce
1 teaspoon brown sugar
1 teaspoon crushed red pepper
Juice of 1 lime
1 tablespoon vegetable oil
12 bamboo skewers

Instructions:
1. Mix all the ingredients except the chicken together in a shallow bowl. Put the chicken pieces in the mix. Place in the refrigerator. Marinate at least 1 hour and preferably overnight.
2. Soak the bamboo skewers in water to keep them from burning. Thread 1 chicken strip onto each skewer. Place on a grill or under a broiler for about 15 minutes or until the chicken is thoroughly cooked—golden outside and white inside. Serve with rice and peanut sauce.

Serves 4

they like, no two bowls of noodles taste exactly the same. Yet every bowl is delicious. Chefs Wandee Young and Byron Ayanoglu explain: "The result is so harmonious, so perfect in every way."[12]

Scrumptious Satay

Satay is another delicious and nutritious snack that Thais love. Rather than describing a particular dish, satay

Peanut Sauce

Satay is always served with a creamy peanut sauce. Peanut sauce also makes a great dipping sauce for shrimp or fried fish. This recipe is easy to make. It uses water for the sauce. For a thicker, creamier sauce, coconut milk can be used.

Ingredients:
½ cup creamy peanut butter
½ cup water
1 teaspoon sugar
1 tablespoon soy sauce
1 tablespoon lime juice
Crushed red pepper to taste

Instructions:
1. Combine the ingredients in a bowl that can be used in a microwave oven. Mix well until they form a smooth sauce.
2. Microwave for 1 minute, or put in a pot and bring to a boil, stirring frequently.
3. Remove the sauce from heat and pour into individual dipping bowls.

Serves 4

describes a method of cooking in which marinated meat is threaded onto bamboo skewers and slowly grilled over hot coals. Cooking meat in this manner probably originated with prehistoric humans. Almost every Asian culture has its own form of satay. Not surprisingly, Thai satay is spicier than that of neighboring countries.

To make satay, Thai cooks marinate pieces of pork, beef, or chicken in a multi-flavored sauce made with nam plah, coconut milk, chili, lime juice, and sugar. Then the meat is threaded onto short bamboo skewers and slowly cooked over hot coals. As it cooks, it is brushed with coconut milk, which tenderizes and sweetens the meat and fills the air with a wonderful aroma.

The meat is served with slices of cucumbers and a mound of fragrant jasmine rice. A sweet and spicy peanut sauce always accompanies it. The result is a hot, juicy treat that is hard to resist. Cooking experts at Temple of Thai, a Web site dedicated to Thai food, explain: "Satay is succulent. . . . It is fun to . . . eat, tasty and highly portable. . . . Its widespread popularity is well deserved."[13]

Fantastic Fruit Treats

Tropical fruits of every size and shape grow all over Thailand. When Thais want a sweet snack, they have dozens of fresh, juicy fruits to pick from. Bananas, mangoes, papayas, watermelons, tiny mandarin oranges, and pineapples are just a few favorites. Vendors slice fresh fruit and put the slices in plastic bags. Each bag contains a bamboo skewer to eat the fruit with and

Stinky Fruit

Durians are unusual tropical fruits that many Thais like to combine with sticky rice and coconut milk for a special treat. These football-sized fruits have brownish green skin covered by sharp spikes. It is necessary to wear gloves when handling durians. But inside, the yellow flesh is sweet and custard like.

It is the fruit's aroma, however, that distinguishes it. Many people say it smells like dirty socks. That is why the fruit has been banned on airplanes and in some public places in Thailand.

Durians grow on trees that can be 130 feet (39.62m) tall and are pollinated by bats. The fruits develop their peculiar scent as they ripen. In fact, the only way to tell if a durian is ripe is by smelling it. Although many people cannot get past a durian's unpleasant fragrance, others love its sweet, creamy flavor.

The spiky durian has a sweet, creamy taste despite its foul smell.

a smaller bag filled with a mixture of chili powder, sugar, lime, and salt. Thais love to dip the fruit into this spicy mix. They also like to combine fruits with other ingredients to create scrumptious sweet snacks. Popular choices include fried bananas and bananas in coconut milk.

Bananas in coconut milk is a soupy treat made by boiling slices of ripe bananas and sugar in coconut milk. Served warm or chilled with a handful of sweet mung beans sprinkled on top, this creamy creation is delicious. And since bananas are loaded with vital vitamins and minerals, it is almost as nutritious as it is tasty.

Bananas are also eaten fried. These delicacies are made by rolling banana slices in a batter of rice flour, sugar, eggs, water, and shredded coconut. The slices are dropped into sizzling hot oil and fried until they are golden brown. The tricky part is making sure that the temperature of the oil is about 375°F (191°C). If the oil is too cool, the fritters do not cook fast enough and absorb too much oil. If it is too hot, the fritters

Bananas in coconut milk can be served warm or cold and is a very nutritious drink.

burn. But when the oil temperature is perfect, the fritters are crisp, sweet, and light. Before the fritters are served, the cook drizzles honey on top.

Apples and Pineapples

Thais so love this sweet snack that they also fry pineapple and apple slices in the same way. These delectable tidbits are sold all over Thailand. According to Thai cooking experts Deh-Ta Hsiung, Becky Johnson, and Sallie Morris: "These deliciously sweet treats are a favorite with children and adults alike in Thailand. You will find them on sale from portable roadside stalls and markets at almost any hour of the day or night."[14]

With sweet, juicy fruit treats, succulent skewers of satay, and delectable noodle dishes being sold everywhere, it is no wonder that Thais love to snack. The many choices are simply irresistible.

Chapter

4

Sharing Food

Sharing food is a key part of Thai culture. Most Thais are Buddhists. Their religion emphasizes generosity. One way that Buddhists show generosity is by sharing food with monks.

Each morning, hundreds of Buddhist monks walk through the streets of Thailand carrying empty bowls that kindly Thais fill with rice and other tasty tidbits. On holidays and special occasions, sweet treats are prepared just for the monks. Once the monks have been fed, celebrating Thais share these delicacies with each other. Many of these treats originated in the past and have special meaning. Among these special foods are sticky rice with mangoes, **krayasart** (kruh-yuh-surt), and golden desserts.

40

Buddhist monks receive food offerings every morning on the streets of Thailand.

Since ancient times, Thais have celebrated **Songkran** (song-kruhn) in April. This four-day new year's festival is both serious and fun. Many Thai cooks spend the first two days of the holiday preparing food to offer the monks on the third day, which is New Year's Day. The most popular offering is sticky rice with mangoes, a sweet and delicious pudding-like treat. Because this dish is so luscious, Thai cooks make enough so that after the monks are fed, there is plenty for family members to enjoy and take along on the fun-filled picnics that mark the final day of Songkran.

A New Year's Treat

It takes time to make sticky rice with mangoes, which is why Thai cooks often start two days in advance. First, the rice is soaked in water for at least four hours, and often overnight. As the rice soaks, it absorbs the water, which softens and plumps it.

While the rice is cooking, the cook prepares a warm, creamy sauce made with coconut milk and sugar. Pandanus leaves, lily leaves that taste and smell like vanilla, add scent and flavor to the sauce. Many cooks also add a drop of jasmine essence, an oil extracted from jasmine flowers, which adds a powerful perfume to the dish.

The hot coconut sauce is poured over the cooked rice, which is left to stand in the rich liquid for about fifteen minutes. This allows each grain of rice to absorb the delicious flavor and fragrance of the sauce. Before serving, the cook adds sweet, juicy mango slices to the rice and more

Celebrating Songkran

One of the most famous parts of the Songkran celebration is the playful throwing of water. Armed with buckets and water hoses, Thai friends splash each other as well as anyone who passes by. This is done all in fun and as a way to wash away the old year. And in order to start the new year free and happy, Thais release caged birds that are sold before Songkran just for this purpose. They also release fish into rivers.

Thai people celebrate Songkran, a new year's festival, by splashing water on each other.

coconut sauce. The dish, which is served warm or at room temperature, is extraordinarily delicious—sweet, aromatic, and creamy. "This one has a fabulous texture (derived from Thai sticky rice, whose grains remain individual though soft after steaming) and a deep coconutty taste. Its accompanying mango slices are a definite bonus,"[15] explains chef David Thompson.

A Crunchy Rice Bar

Songkran is not the only holiday during which Thais prepare special dishes to honor the monks and share with each other. Every autumn, people throughout Asia celebrate the rice harvest with a big festival. Because Thailand is in the tropics, autumn is not harvest time there. But that does not stop clever Thais from celebrating. Thai farmers plant a special type of flat rice, that can be harvested at this time. It is used to make a treat known as krayasart that is offered to the monks on Sart Day.

Krayasart is a delectable concoction that looks and tastes like a granola bar. It is made with seven ingredients: flat rice, puffed rice, peanuts, sugar, honey, sesame seeds, and coconut milk. Since Thais consider seven a lucky number, eating krayasart is thought to bring good luck. Thais have been making this sweet and crunchy treat for centuries. In ancient times, it was prepared by young women who spent hours stirring huge kettles that were placed

Sticky Rice with Mango

Glutinous or sticky rice can be purchased in Asian grocery stores and in many supermarkets. Use sweet, ripe mangoes.

Ingredients:
1 cup cooked sticky rice
$\frac{3}{4}$ cup + 4 tablespoons coconut milk
2 tablespoons sugar
2 ripe mangoes, peeled and cut into slices
$\frac{1}{4}$ teaspoon salt

Instructions:
1. Cook the sticky rice as directed on the package.
2. Combine $\frac{3}{4}$ cup coconut milk, sugar, and salt and mix well.
3. Pour the coconut milk mixture over the rice. Stir well. Let stand 15 minutes.
4. Put the rice in 4 bowls. Arrange the mango slices on the sides of the bowls. Pour the remaining coconut milk on top, 1 tablespoon per bowl.

Serves 4

Thai farmers harvest rice, a staple ingredient for main dishes and desserts.

in the center of every village. Once the ingredients formed a sticky paste, it was placed on trays to harden, then sliced and wrapped in banana leaves. Back then, the best krayasart was offered to both the king and Buddhist monks. Bars of krayasart were also left on roadsides, where wandering ghosts could find them.

Today, many Thais prepare krayasart at home, while others buy the chewy treat ready-made. On Sart, Thais take krayasart to the many temples that dot the landscape. Here, they pile the bars in resident monks' bowls, which have been carefully lined up on raised platforms just for the occasion. Once the bowls are overflowing, friends and neighbors exchange krayasart. This gives everyone a chance to share, spread good luck, and taste each other's recipes. A Thai man recalls this practice: "People would exchange the remaining krayasart among themselves. In so doing, they could have the opportunity to test krayasart cooked by others. As a result, anyone whose krayasart had an excellent taste would have his good name spread mouth-to-mouth."[16]

Golden Desserts

Other sweets, known as golden desserts, are also offered to monks during religious ceremonies and they are shared with friends and family members at weddings. These sweet delicacies have the Thai word for "gold," thong (tawng), in their names. Sharing these desserts signifies that the newlywed couple, the monks who bless the wedding, and the guests will have rich lives.

Zesty Fruit Slices

On the last day of Songkran, many Thais go on a picnic. Slices of fresh fruit with multi-flavored dipping powder are popular picnic snacks. Any fruit can be used. This recipe uses apple slices.

Ingredients:
2 large apples, washed, cored, and cut into 8 slices each
1/2 cup sugar
1/4 cup chili powder
2 teaspoons salt
Juice of 1 lemon

Instructions:
1. Pour half of the lemon juice over the apple slices to keep them from turning brown.
2. Place the apple slices in 4 plastic zippered bags, 4 slices per bag.
3. Mix the sugar, chili powder, and salt together. Slowly add the remaining lemon juice and mix well. It will form a paste.
4. Divide the paste into the four zippered bags.

Serves 4

Another Way of Sharing

Early Thai kings were famous for the fabulous banquets that were served in their palaces. But while people shared food at these banquets, modern Thais hold a special banquet for monkeys. This event takes place in Lop Buri, a village north of Bangkok. The village and surrounding area is famous for the hundreds of macaques (long-tailed monkeys) that live there.

Once a year the people of Lop Buri prepare dozens of rice and fruit dishes that they share with the animals. The food is placed on long tables. The monkeys, who are unafraid of humans, jump on the tables and feast.

Once a year, macaques share food with people in the town of Lop Buri.

There are a number of golden desserts. Two of the most popular are thong yib (tawng yib), or pinched gold, and phoy thong (foy tawng), or gold string. The main ingredients in both are sugar, coconut milk, and duck egg yolks. Thais believe that the more important the occasion, the more egg yolks a dish must contain, and most golden desserts contain at least a dozen. Thais did not

Fresh cooked food is served hot at a busy streetside restaurant in Bangkok.

start making these bright yellow sweets until the 16th century, when Portuguese visitors introduced Thais to cooking with eggs. No one knows whether Thai cooks invented golden desserts or adapted them from Portuguese recipes. Whatever the case, artistic Thai chefs have made these delicacies their own.

Skillful Cooking

Making thong yib and phoy thong is not easy. First, cooks make a hot, sticky syrup from sugar and coconut milk. Next, they beat the egg yolks until they are smooth and creamy. To make thong yib, the cook ladles the egg yolk into the hot syrup. As the mixture starts to set, but before it can harden, the cook carefully removes a bit at a time, forming spheres with pinched or pleated edges. These are dropped into tiny cups to cool.

Making phoy thong takes even more skill. Using a pastry tube, the cook trickles the egg mixture into the syrup, where it forms golden threads similar to cotton candy. The threads are then carefully swirled around until a pyramid or a spiral emerges. Skilled Thai cooks pile these pyramids together on a platter to look like a **wai** (way), the traditional Thai sign of respect in which a person presses his or her two hands together in a prayer-like position. The results are elegant and tasty, but difficult to achieve. Jennifer Brennan explains: "I have seen a Thai cook deftly trickle the egg threads into perfect skeins, arranging them in smooth little cushions with the aid of chopsticks. The first time I tried it mine looked like a bird's nest assembled by an absent minded sparrow."[17]

But even when made by beginners, these golden desserts taste wonderful. Sharing these sweet delicacies, along with krayasart and sticky rice and mangoes, gives Thais a chance to open their hearts to others. The delicious taste of these treats and the joy of giving combine to make special days more memorable and fun.

Metric Conversions

Mass (Weight)

1 ounce (oz.)	= 28.0 grams (g)
8 ounces	= 227.0 grams
1 pound (lb.) or 16 ounces	= 0.45 kilograms (kg)
2.2 pounds	= 1.0 kilogram

Liquid Volume

1 teaspoon (tsp.)	= 5.0 milliliters (ml)
1 tablespoon (tbsp.)	= 15.0 milliliters
1 fluid ounce (oz.)	= 30.0 milliliters
1 cup (c.)	= 240 milliliters
1 pint (pt.)	= 480 milliliters
1 quart (qt.)	= 0.95 liters (l)
1 gallon (gal.)	= 3.80 liters

Pan Sizes

8-inch cake pan	= 20 x 4-centimeter cake pan
9-inch cake pan	= 23 x 3.5-centimeter cake pan
11 x 7-inch baking pan	= 28 x 18-centimeter baking pan
13 x 9-inch baking pan	= 32.5 x 23-centimeter baking pan
9 x 5-inch loaf pan	= 23 x 13-centimeter loaf pan
2-quart casserole	= 2-liter casserole

Temperature

212° F	= 100° C (boiling point of water)
225° F	= 110° C
250° F	= 120° C
275° F	= 135° C
300° F	= 150° C
325° F	= 160° C
350° F	= 180° C
375° F	= 190° C
400° F	= 200° C

Length

$1/4$ inch (in.)	= 0.6 centimeters (cm)
$1/2$ inch	= 1.25 centimeters
1 inch	= 2.5 centimeters

Notes

Chapter 1: Land of Plenty

1. Quoted in Joe Cummings, *World Food: Thailand*. Victoria, Australia: Lonely Planet, 2000, p. 19.

2. Kasma Loha-unchit, *It Rains Fishes*. San Francisco: Pomegranate Artbooks, 1995, p. 24.

3. Jennifer Brennan, *Thai Cookbook*. New York: Perigee, 1981, p. 176.

4. Kasma Loha-unchit, "Flavoring Food with Fish Sauce," Thai Food and Travel. www.thaifoodandtravel.com/features/fish sauce2.html.

5. Quoted in Cummings, *World Food,* p. 79.

Chapter 2: Delicious Flavors

6. Brennan, *Thai Cookbook,* p. 126.

7. Quoted in Wen Zientek-Sico, "Thai Curry—Adding Flavors of Thailand to Your Table Tablespoon by Tablespoon," Regional Recipes. www.regionalrecipes.com/article1020html.

8. David Thompson, *Thai Food*. Berkeley, CA: Ten Speed, 2002, p. 336.

9. Brennan, *Thai Cookbook,* p. 122.

10. Kasma Loha-unchit, *It Rains Fishes,* p. 98.

Chapter 3: Snacks and More Snacks

11. Cummings, *World Food,* p. 199.

12. Wandee Young and Byron Ayanoglu, *Simply Thai Cooking.* Toronto, Canada: Robert Rose, 2003, p. 75.

13. Temple of Thai, "Satay." www.templeofthai.com/cooking/about_satay.php.

14. Deh-Ta Hsiung, Becky Johnson, and Sallie Morris, *Thai.* New York: Barnes & Noble, 2004, p. 460.

Chapter 4: Sharing Food

15. Thompson, *Thai Food,* p. 617.

16. Khonkaen Link, "Sart Day." www.khonkaenlink.com/forum/forum_posts.asp?TID=813&PN=1.

17. Brennan, *Thai Cookbook,* p. 257.

Glossary

Bangkok: The capital of Thailand.

curry: A paste made from herbs and spices and cooked in a liquid in which various foods are added.

gaeng: The Thai word for "curry."

garnishes: Toppings or trimmings that are added to food.

krayasart: A Thai sweet made with nuts and honey, popular during autumn.

mortar: A stone bowl used for making curry paste.

nam plah: A fish sauce that Thais use like salt.

nam prik: A popular dipping sauce that mixes nam plah, shrimp paste, roasted red chilies, garlic, lime juice, and sugar.

pad thai: A popular stir-fried noodle dish.

pestle: A small clublike tool used to pound herbs and spices into curry paste.

prawns: Large shrimps.

satay: A method of cooking in which marinated meat is threaded onto bamboo skewers and grilled over hot coals.

Songkran: Thai New Year, celebrated on April 13.

stock: A liquid made by cooking vegetables, meat, bones, poultry, or fish in boiling water.

wai: A traditional Thai symbol of respect, greeting, and parting, in which a person presses his or her hands together in a prayer-like position and bows the head.

yam: The Thai word for "salad."

For Further Exploration

Books

Arlette Braman, *Kids Around the World Cook! The Best Foods and Recipes from Many Lands.* New York: Wiley, 2000. This book has recipes and food facts from many different countries and includes a section on Thailand.

Matthew Locricchio, *The Cooking of Thailand.* New York: Benchmark, 2004. A kid's cookbook with nice pictures.

Devagi Sanmugam, *Fun with Asian Food: A Kid's Cookbook.* Singapore: Periplus Editions, 2005. An Asian cookbook that includes Thai dishes.

Web Sites

Enjoy Thai Food (www.enjoythaifood.com). A Thai food blog with dozens of interesting articles, including articles about school lunches, and many recipes.

Maps 4 Kids—Thailand Travel (www.map4kids.com/world/asia/thailand/index.php). This Web site has a detailed map of Thailand plus a virtual tour of the country through photos.

Thailand, Asia for Kids (www.afk.com/resources/countryfacts/thailand). This Web site gives a map and information on Thailand's geography, history, people, and government.

Thailand Life (www.thailandlife.com). A Thai teenager tells about his life with information about Thai food, culture, religion, and daily life. There are lots of photos and links to other sites.

Index

anchovies, 11–12
appearance, of food, 25
aroma, 37
Ayanoglu, Byron, 35

banana chilies, 15, 20
bananas, 38–39
banquets, for monkeys, 49
bean and thread noodles, 31
beef salad, 23, 24
bird's eye chilies, 14–15
black sticky rice, 31
Brennan, Jennifer
  on fish and seafood, 11
  on making curry paste, 19
  on soup, 24
  on wai, 51
Buddhism, 40

chicken and coconut soup, 26
chicken satay, 34
children, 13

chili peppers, 12–15, 20, 38
Chinese immigrants, 29, 31
coconut milk
  in banana snacks, 38
  in curry sauce, 19, 20
  in peanut sauce, 35
  in snacks, 31
  soup with, 26
  in sticky rice with mangoes, 42, 45
cooking methods
  for bananas, 38–39
  for curry paste, 19–20
  for fish and seafood, 11
  for golden desserts, 51
  for krayasart, 44, 47
  for lemongrass, 7
  for noodles, 32
  for rice, 8, 9
  for satays, 36
  see also recipes
Cummings, Joe, 28
curries, 15, 16, 19–20

desserts, 47, 49, 51
dry noodles, 32
durians, 37

eating utensils, 18
egg noodles, 31
eggs, 49, 51

fish
  importance of, 10–11
  sauces from, 11–12, 19–20
  in soup, 24, 27
food, as art, 25
food sharing
  golden desserts and, 47, 49, 51
  religious tradition of, 40
  Sart Day and, 44, 47
  Songkran and, 42–44, 45, 48
food vendors, 28–29
fruit, 36–39, 48
gaeng. *See* curries

Gaeng Chud Look Cheen (fish ball and

mushroom soup), 24

garnishes, 23, 32, 35

glutinous rice. *See* sticky rice

golden desserts, 47, 49, 51

green curry, 20

green papaya salad, 24

greens, 22

harvest festival, 44, 47

holiday foods, 42–45, 47, 48

hot and sour prawn soup, 27

Hsiung, Deh-Ta, 39

jasmine rice, 8, 9

Johnson, Becky, 39

krayasart, 44, 47

lemongrass, 7
  in curries, 20
  in salads, 23
  in soup, 24, 26

Loha-unchit, Kasma
  on fish sauce, 12
  on hot and sour prawn soup, 27
  on rice, 8

Lop Buri (Thailand), 49

luck, 44

macaques, 49

mangoes, 40, 42–44, 45

massaman curry, 20

monkey banquets, 49

monks, sharing food with
  golden desserts and, 47, 49, 51
  religious tradition of, 40
  Sart Day and, 44, 47
  Songkran and, 42–44, 45, 48

Morris, Sallie, 39

mortars, 19

mung beans, 31

nam pla, 11–12, 19–20

nam prik, 12

napkins, 18

noodles, 29, 31–32, 35

nuts, 14

orange curry, 20

pad thai, 32

peanut sauce, 35

pestles, 19

phoy thong (gold string dessert), 49, 51

picnics, 48

Pornipitatong, Patchara, 20

Portuguese traders, 12–13, 51

prawn soup, 27

recipes
  beef salad, 23
  chicken and co-conut soup, 26
  chicken satay, 34
  hot and sweet nuts, 14
  jasmine rice, 9
  peanut sauce, 35
  sticky rice with mangoes, 45
  zesty fruit slices, 48

red curry, 20

religion, 40

rice
  harvest festival for, 44
  importance of, 4, 6, 8, 10
  noodles from, 31
  soup and, 24
  sticky, 31, 40, 42–44, 45

salads, 20, 22–24

Sart Day, 44, 47

satays, 34, 35–36

sauces
  fish, 11–12, 19–20

peanut, 35
salad dressings, 22
see also curries
seafood. *See* fish
shrimp paste. *See*
  nam pla
sky-pointing chilies,
  15
snacks, 28–29, 31–32,
  34–39, 48
Songkran, 42–44, 45,
48
soups, 24, 26–27
sticky rice, 31, 40,
  42–44, 45
stinky fruit, 37
stir-fried noodles, 32
stock, for soup, 24

table manners, 18, 31
Thompson, David,
  22, 44
thong yib (pinched
  gold dessert), 49, 51

wai, 51
weddings, 47
wet noodles, 32

yam, 20, 22–24
Young, Wandee, 35

Picture Credits

Cover image: © Dave Bartruff, Inc./CORBIS
Bernard Napthine/Lonely Planet Images, 43
Bill Aron/PhotoEdit, 38
© Bohemian Nomad Picturemakers/CORBIS, 6
© Catherine Karnow/CORBIS, 21
Corel Corporation, 22 (top)
© Dean Conger/CORBIS, 13
Food Pix/Getty Images, 7, 45
Iconica/Getty Images, 30
James Marshall/CORBIS, 49
Jerry Alexander/Lonely Planet Images, 18
Joe Cummings/Lonely Planet Images, 33, 41
John Hulme; Eye Ubiquitous/CORBIS, 10
Joseph Paris, 22 (bottom), 26, 34, 48
Lonely Planet/Getty Images, 46
© Macduff Everton/CORBIS, 29, 37
Maury Aaseng, 5
PhotoDisc, 12 (top and bottom), 44
© Richard T. Nowitz/CORBIS, 25
Robert Harding World Imagery/Getty Images, 50
Royalty-Free/SuperStock, 9
StockFood/Getty Images, 17

About the Author

Barbara Sheen is the author of numerous works of fiction and nonfiction for young people. She lives in New Mexico with her family. In her spare time, she likes to swim, walk, garden, and read. And, of course, she loves to cook!